ABRAHAM

AFRICANUS I.

His Secret Life,

AS REVEALED UNDER THE

MESMERIC INFLUENCE.

Mysteries of the White House.

J. F. FEEKS, PUBLISHER,

No. 26 ANN STREET, N. Y.

ABRAHAM

AFRICANUS I.

His Secret Life,

AS REVEALED UNDER THE

MESMERIC INFLUENCE.

Mysteries of the White House.

J. F. FEEKS, PUBLISHER,
No. 26 ANN STREET, N. Y.

ABRAHAM

AFRICANUS I.

TO THE READER.

Immortal Truth! thy power essay
To lash the morals of the day,
And should the Muse's efforts claim
Small honor for an humble name,
Her aim is gained, by thee directed,
If but one rascal be detected.

Great knaves deserve thy lash the most,
Because they sin at greatest cost,
And every sin thou dost forgive,
Will in a hundred, meaner live,
Till multitudes will boldly ape
The greater one, should he escape.

Man is my theme, yet when I choose
A playful measure for my Muse,
Forget not, Reader, I design
To make the graver censure thine;
Forget not, as I paint for you
Revolting scenes as droll as true,
I claim this judgment still for them,
That, tho' you smile, you do condemn.

Chapter I.

THE GREAT MAN'S FRIEND.

One stormy night in chill November,
As cold a night as folks remember,
'Twas ten o'clock and every street
Was cold and damp with rain and sleet
Old chimneys rocked and tiles were cast
At mercy of the fitful blast ;
And houses shook and shutters slammed,
And stray curs yelpt and hackmen damned ;
And tavern signs were heard to creak
As if their very hearts would break,
And leafless trees swayed to and fro
As if they'd nothing else to do,
Still grew the darkness, deep, profound,
O'er roof and dome and all around,
And froze the rain, and moaned the blast
Like gibbering spirits as it passed.
Each straggler hugged his friendly cloak,
As home his lonely way he took,
While all the smiles which blessed his home
Seem'd brighter 'mid the deep'ning gloom ;
And oft he started as he passed,
At shadows which the street lamp cast ;—
The sleeping watchman snug and tight
Forgot to hail the passing night ;
And wind and rain and driving sleet
Soon held possession of the street.

Within his arm-chair, snug and warm,
Bram, dozing sat, nor heard the storm,
Or, if he heard, he thought, no doubt,
How very cold it must be, out.
The warm full bed and cozy curtain
Made pleasant rest and slumber certain ;
And the warm arm chair, as you'll suppose,
Seemed almost courting him to doze.
Within the broad hearth where he gazed,

A gladsome fire cracked and blazed,
And rose and fell with cheering sound,
Dispensing light and heat around.
The clothes he wore and all his pride,
Were both together laid aside,
And in his night gown, at his ease,
He felt his comfort much increase ;
Small care had he for rain or snows ;
His Excellency viewed his toes,
And took his punch, as grateful heat
Came running through his lanky feet.
Bram warmed his toes and sipped his liquor,
Until his thoughts and tongue grew thicker ;
Nor could he think, small brains he boasted,
Whether his feet were warmed or roasted.
Thus in his mind confusion grew
Until he neither thought nor knew ;
Yet, tho' he slept, his master mind,
(These common folks are always blind)
Beheld what passed. "What's that I see?
The very andiron bows to me !"
And so it was ; the andiron grew
Beneath his Excellency's view,
And as it grew he could but note
Its brass arms stuck beneath its coat ;
He wondered if 'twould next have wings,
For rum and dreams can do strange things.
"Great God !" quoth Bram, "what do I see?
The very andiron bows to me!"

"Yes, Bram," quoth it, "I bow ; you'll find
A fellow feeling makes us kind.
I am the Devil, and I feel
Of all the rogues who wrong, who steal,
Who murder, intrigue, violate,
I love the rogue who rules a State,
Because, when he does wrong or says it,
A thousand knaves and fools must praise it,
And all the efforts preachers make
Will not avail, 'tis bound to take ;
I love you, Bram, your high position

Gives hope to knaves of mean condition,
When gazing on your strange success,
They think their own fate can't be less
Make 't easy men should find a flaw
In codes of morals and of law ;
And on their wits in firm reliance,
Set all of virtue at defiance ;
They think that he who like yourself,
Concentres all and all in self,
Will find that fate and luck conspire,
Both, that the knave may rise the higher,
Both, that a strange success in life,
May be of knave, fool, fortune, rife ;
That Justice, being blind, must lag ;
That Luck's by far the fastest nag,
And on her back in hope they 'll vault,
To carry Fortune by assault.
This serves my ends. It proves when past,
Knave, fool, and fortune, all won't last,
And while it hides the sure defeat,
Mine is the profit and the cheat ;
I've ruled the world and still must rule
As long as there's a knave and fool."

"Stop, stop," cried guilty Bram, "suppose
Instead of jingling verse we chat in prose."

"Agreed" said Satan, ' though its my conviction
You 'll find the prose as difficult to face as fiction."

"Well, the fact is," said Abraham, handing old Nick a chair and pushing the decanter towards him, "it comes more natural. I can defend myself a good deal easier ; your word to the contrary notwithstanding. This reminds me of a western story."

"Ah," said Satan, pouring himself out a pretty stiff horn and gazing at the fire through its amber transparency with the air of a connoisseur, "a joke ?"

"Yes, what I should call a d——n good joke, for it served my purpose elegantly."

"Don't swear;" interrupted Nick, "forget your old habits for once, and behave yourself while in the presence of a gentleman *as* a gentleman."

"'Twas a big thing on Douglas, though; I assure you," continued Abe.

"Douglas, Douglas," said the Devil reflectively, "don't know him."

"What! not the Little Giant of the West? I thought he had gone to ——*you*, long ago."

"'Mistake, my dear boy; he must have gone the other way, for I havn't seen him in our direction."

"Well, well," said Abraham, "no matter. Here's the story: During the electioneering campaign I had with Douglas in Illinois, we agreed to debate our differences in public. On the occasion of the first debate which took place at Ottowa, the Judge asked me a number of questions which he had written down on a piece of paper. Among them were the following:

[Q. 2.] I desire Lincoln to answer whether he stands *pledged* to-day as he did in 1854 against the admission of any more slave States into the Union, even if the people want them?

[Q. 3.] I want to know whether Lincoln stands pledged against the admission of a new State into the Union, with such a Constitution as the people of that State may see fit to make?

[Q. 4.] I want to know whether he stands to-day pledged to the abolition of slavery in the District of Columbia?"

"Pretty good for the Judge," cried Satan, polishing off the end of his tail with his pocket-handkerchief. "I don't see how you managed to get round them."

"Easy enough, my boy," says Abraham, tipping his friend the wink, "I didn't answer them at all!"

"Then he defeated you in the debate?"

"Not at all. I *promised* to answer them at the next debate at Freeport."

"Ha! ha! very good," cried Satan, "promises are an easy means to appease. You promised to end the war in ninety days for instance. *The walls of my abode are covered with them.* But how did you manage the Judge at Freeport?"

"You shall hear," said Abe, exultingly. "When I appeared on the stand I had my answers all ready in writing. They were as follows:

[Ans. 2.] I do not now, nor ever did, stand *pledged* against the admission of any more slave States into the Union.

[Ans. 3.] I do not stand *pledged* against the admission of a new State into the Union, with such a Constitution as the people of that State may see fit to make.

[Ans. 4.] I do not stand *to-day* *pledged* to the abolition of slavery in the District of Columbia."

Bram was silent. The Devil twitched nervously on his chair, turning over the blade of his tail with a troubled air, as though by so doing he hoped to find the *point*.

"I confess," said Nick, " *I don't see the point !*"

"Plain enough;" said Bram, putting his arms round his friend's neck and speaking in a tone of exultation. "I said, 'my friends, the Judge shall be answered strictly in accordance with the interrogatories he has put to me. *I do not stand* PLEDGED *to anything !*'"*

---

*See Debate at Freeport, Illinois.

"Bully for you," cried Satan, enraptured, "you are the smartest pupil I ever had! I am afraid people will find you out after a while, though."

"Devil a fear, Old Boy. *As long as I'm called 'Honest Old Abe,' the people will swallow anything. There's nothing like having an honest name. It is a cloak for everything.*"

"True;" said Beelzebub. He forbore to say any more. His mind was filled with uneasy suspicions. What if the cute Bram should slip out of his bargain with *him?* "True," he continued, rolling this idea over in his mind; "if I hadn't tacked this name to you, you would have been nowhere to-day. It gave *confidence*, and you've profited well by it. But how about *our* arrangement. You don't expect to argue *me* out of *that*, do you?"

"Come, come, brother," said Bram with an affected air of honest indignation. "You don't suspect my *intentions* do you?"

"Hell is paved with them," said the Father of Lies, sententiously. "I want something more palpable than your assurances, Abe. Suppose we draw up a little memorandum of our agreement?"

So saying, he whipped out a little scroll of parchment, and tapping a hole in Bram's arm before he was sufficiently aware of his intention to prevent it, used his blood for ink. Then scribbling furiously for a few minutes, he covered the scroll with fine writing, and read the contract to his *confrere:*

"'I hereby pledge to elevate Abraham Lincoln to a life Presidency of the United States of America——'"

"Stop, stop!" cried Bram, "you promised a Monarchy, or at least a First Consulship."

"Fool!" said the Devil. "Don't you perceive that if you call yourself a King or First Consul, the whole people will rise upon you?"

"Let them rise," said Bram, " I have my army. Every officer has been selected and appointed with that view. They are all men who believe the government needs to be *strengthened*."

"Your army wouldn't be worth a straw if you proceed so rudely. There are democrats enough in the country to eat up your army."

"But they're not organized," urged Bram, "and what's more, I don't intend to let them organize."

"Very strongly put, brother; but still there's nothing like doing things smoothly. My word for it, the easiest way is the best. You owe all your present success to four things. *First*, MY NOMINATION. *Second*, Your sobriquet of 'Honest.' *Third*, Those weak points of the Constitution which a little management converted into flaws, and a little stretching widened into fissures wide enough to drive a train of cars through. 'Military necessity' did the rest. *Fourth*, DOING THINGS QUIETLY. All these things combined have given you what I promised you in our first contract, POWER. In return you brought on a war which has made, taking both belligerents together, something like a million of victims.

"And out of that million," chuckled Abe, "of course, you reaped a plentiful harvest."

"Not so, Bram. I never was more deceived in my life. I GOT MY SHARE; but the majority of them were poor ignorant fools, infused with a false patriotism. I did well with the Abolitionists, and the men who accepted bounties; but the former were very scarce and the latter were hardly worth picking up. But to our contract. If you 're elected for another term, you can easily get a law passed declaring the country in a state of permanent insurrection, and demanding more power to put it down. The first thing will be, a law to make the Presidency perpetual while the war lasts: the next, another making it perpetual during your life. Thus you will have got over the hardest part of it. The rest is easy enough. You can then have it entailed on your posterity, and change the title whenever you please. I should advise you to stick to that of President, though. There's nothing like a mild name. To continue :

'I hereby pledge to elevate Abraham Lincoln to a life Presidency of the United States of America, and to stand by him and assist him to subvert the liberties of the American people and debauch their civic aspirations; to impose upon them in every imaginable form of low cunning, and cheat them with words of double meaning and with false promises, until by these, and kindred means, that end is accomplished, and his dynasty firmly established.' "

While Satan was writing the contract, Bram held out his arm very patiently by way of inkstand ; but now he withdrew it hastily, and looking at his watch, exclaimed :

" All right, my boy, I 'll sign that, and then you'll please to consider this interview at an end, for some of my generals have been advancing too quickly, and if I don't relieve them of their commands the war will be over in a jiffy, and good-bye to my plans."

" You forget," said Beelzebub meaningly, and fixed his burning eyes upon Bram's, till the latter winced and wiggled as though he was on a toasting fork, "you forget, my dear Bram."

"What?" stammered Bram, fearing he had been detected, yet hoping to escape, "What do I forget?"

"What!" roared the Evil One, "Do you pretend you don't know! you low, cunning, pettifogging, cringing, artful, Illinois stump lawyer! Would you cheat *me*? You know very well *there's no considera-tion expressed in that deed*, or you wouldn't have been in such a hurry to sign it, and run to look after your major-generals. But come, let us remain friends. I admire you the more for your dishonesty; only you musn't think to 'beat the Devil round a stump. Honor amongst thieves, you know."

So saying, the worthy pair shook hands and *smiled*. The *elder one* then proceeded to finish the agreement:

"'In consideration whereof my friend promises, (no —pledges,) pledges to render unto me what he pos-sesses (it ain't much, any how,) of a MORTAL SOUL, the same to be MINE forever!

(Signed)   BAAL."

(Signed)   BRAM."

"Now," said Baal, as Old Abe with trembling fingers and face white as a sheet, signed the bond; "now, my dear Abe, if you want any advice, just let me know, for like yourself, I've other matters to at-tend to."

"Don't be in a hurry," said Abe, looking with re-gret upon the parchment which Baal had suffered to remain on the table, "what shall I do with the Aboli-tion party? Nothing I do seems to please them. Phillips is constantly abusing me"

"Issue a Proclamation of Emancipation. You remember you said at Chicago, July 10, 1858, 'I hate, and have always hated slavery as much as any other Abolitionist.' It will run well with your words."

"You've a good memory, Nick; but your advice is rather late. I've issued such a Proclamation already."

"The deuce you have! who put you up to that, Abey?"

"It was original, old fellow, original, every line of it."

"Come, come, friend," said Old Nick reproachfully, "you know you havn't brains enough to stretch a clothes line. Somebody must have put you up to it or you never could have done it. Who was it? Sumner?"

"No."

"Hale?"

"No."

"Wilson?"

"Well, Wilson gave me a hint or two."

"Exactly, and upon that hint you spoke."

"Wasn't a bad idea, was it?"

"No! Still you may lose the support of the Conservatives."

"I've provided against that. I issued secret instructions to Banks and others, to pay no attention to the proclamation, and to order the negroes in their respective departments, to remain on their plantations."*

"Well, what good will that do?"

---

*See Banks' General Order Jan. 19, 1864.

"Don't you see? By compelling them to remain, they will be *obliged to work* ——."

"But that's slavery again.

"True, but it won't appear so. We say it is necessary to the public peace that the negroes shall not be roaming about the country. That keeps them at work, and while their labor benefits the men I have appointed to cultivate the plantations, all of whom are creatures of mine, the measure will give assurance to the Conservatives that I am not in a hurry to emancipate."

"Not so bad. I trace brother Seward's mind in that arrangement. But to the Abolitionists again. I don't exactly see what you can do for them, although I understand the value of their support at the elections. How would a draft for half a million more men do?"

"You frighten me. What! half a million more?"

"Yes. It would have a threefold advantage. 1*st*, Please the radicals. 2*d*, Draw away so many votes from the opposition. 3*d*, Convert enemies into friends, for once in the army they'd have no chance for Democratic sentiments."

Bram here slyly covered the scribbled parchment with his long bony hands, but the Devil had been watching him, and caught it up in time. Bram appeared not to be aware of the manœuver, but continued the subject of a proposed draft.

"I like your advice, and shall act upon it. But would'nt such an act be treachery to the States that have filled up the last quota, and treachery to those that were given to suppose there would be no other draft?"

"Bram," said the Devil with a curse,
And dropping prose—relapsing into verse,
"It little becomes either you or I,
To pause at acts of treachery.
Since in the end if there be shame,
We both of us have often been to blame.
Your treason but extends to States,
Mine to a Higher cause relates.
You grasp at POWER; I did the same;
The treason differs but in name."

The Devil vanished as he spoke,
While clouds of ashes and of smoke,
Flew up the chimney in delight,
As if to aid his sudden flight.
Bram rubbed his eyes, and looked to see
The Devil in reality.
Could he have dreamed, or was it true?
The old brass andiron met his view,
And in the hearth burned dim and low,
The fire which was flick'ring, now;
A strange dull feeling in his head,
Warned him 'twas time to go to bed,
With tottering steps he sought his rest,
Where soon he snored as 't may be guessed;
He snored away, and any fellow
Might do the same, who got as mellow.

Chapter II.

THE CONSPIRACY.

SCENE.—*The Smoking Room in the White House.*—CHEEZE *and*
STENTOR *discovered in conversation.*

Enter, BRAM *and* SOO, (*the great Irrepressible Magician.*)

BRAM.

Good friends, to banish public cares,
The mighty Soo with us appears,

And hath engaged to please us so,
In that he purposes to do :
We have consented he shall steep
Our senses in mesmeric sleep,
So that the past and future rise,
As he may will, before our eyes ;
And by clairvoyance clearly view,
Each scene or transit we pass thro'.

CHEEZE AND STENTOR, TOGETHER.

Haste thou, great Soo, your power essay,
In feats not furnished every day.
For us who know your skill in feats,
Of vaultings, tumblings, somersets,
There's little fear that we may doubt,
Should you turn Bram just inside out.

SOO.

Great Sirs, I do not seek to addle,
Your brain with long unmeaning twaddle,
Nor by abstractions infinite,
Your minds to puzzle or benight ;
But by some strong unchallenged facts,
Give truth and credence to my acts,
So that the science and the man,
May challenge doubt, if doubt you can.
Till then, we all must silence keep,
The while I charm Great Bram to sleep.
Then seating Bram upon a chair,
The mighty Soo began to stare ,
Whilst watching both with anxious eye,
The other two stood wondering by.
Thus, long they stood, till Soo advancing,
His eye with magic meaning glancing,
He stood beside, then wildly throwing
His arms about, began pow-wowing ;
Till Bram's great eyes were seen to wink,
His head to nod and forward sink—
Then with a smile to those around,
Great Soo announced the sleep profound.
Invited both to touch and scan,
And then to this effect began :—

You see that all's not what't appears,
To smell, touch, taste, or eyes, or ears,
And many wondrous things may be,
Which baffle our philosophy ;
So Mesmer's magic sleep defies
Hands, nose, and mouth, and ears, and eyes.
He sleeps, and forthwith I'll commence
To act upon his slumbering sense,
And thro' each phrenologic bump,
Act on the brain with moral pump ;
By touching each we'll make appear,
The trait that's hid beneath each hair ;
Of good or ill, we'll have it shown,
And first we'll place our touch on 'Tune.'

Soo here proceeded where he said,
To place his hand upon Bram's head,
Who answering to the magic touch,
Straightway broke out into this snatch :

BRAM.

Retrospectivo piu alleghressimo.

AIR.—"*John Brown.*"

"We'll hang Jeff Davis on a sour apple tree,
We'll hang Jeff Davis on a sour apple tree,
We'll hang Jeff Davis on a sour apple tree,
        As we go marching along! !"

Hold! hold! cried Cheeze and Stentor ; hold:
That song grows hateful as't grows old!
For party purposes it had its day—
We pray thee, wondrous Soo, to change the lay.

BRAM.

Prospectivo fortissimo.

"Oh carry me back,
Oh carry me back,
    To ole Virginny shore ;
I'll change my ways,
And reappoint Mac,
And never do so no more!"

Then shifting his position on the chair,
Great Abram cleared his throat and changed the air :—

BRAM.

Andante jollisimo.

"Come back! come back! we'll vote for Mac,
    Success where'er he goes,
We'll drink to-day, as well we may,
    Confusion to his foes !"

The Greenback Chief with threatening frown,
Upon the sleeping Bram looked down—
While Soo himself, perplexed and puzzled,
Pow-wowed in vain to get him muzzled ;
Nor did succeed 'till one or two
More jolly songs were thus got thro'.
Great Sirs, quoth the Magician, grinning,
I fear my art, not I's been sinning,
In calling secret feelings forth,
Of doubtful use and little worth ·
But if forgiven, I'll instead
Proceed again to touch his head.

The Greenback Chief with smile resigned,
And willing ear his head inclined,
And trembling Stentor dreading worse,
Expressed himself as not averse.
With this the skillful conjurer struck
On "Self-esteem," when forth he broke

BRAM.

Thrice lucky Bram, thy destiny,
The Fates have made for ever high,
As upwards still thy fate to rise,
Success for e'er shall glad thine eyes.
Heaven's own especial favorite thou,
Called Honest Bram where'er you go ;
Gaze on the past and learn from thence,
How well thou'st earned thy recompense ;
Gaze on the future still as kind,
In promise to thy master mind.
From western flat-boats, doomed to toil,
Thy back to bend, thy hands to soil,

Thy fitness for this occupation
Inspired thee to rule the nation ;
And what if nature's freak denied thee brains,
Thou had'st the tact to use thy friends.
To have thyself dubbed "Honest," thy reign a "Mission,"
By simply advocating Abolition.

CHEEZE.

Something too much of this, great Soo,
I cry thee quits, we've something more to do ;
These vaunting boasts can profit naught,
Nor serve in any way our thought ;
But if by arts possessed you can,
In any way confess this man,
Take from him in his slumbering state,
His mental guards, and make him prate ;
Tell whom he trusts and whom he doubts,
What his designs towards "INS" and "OUTS ;"
Whom he will favor, who oppose,
Who thinks his friends, and who his foes,
Who he will aid and who refuse,
And what his own ambitious views—
I'm free to say, my friends and I,
Will be obliged eternally.

SOO.

To do this well upon compunction,
I'll put yourself in close conjunction ;
By proxy make thee act magician,
And touch the bump of his Ambition ;
Which having done, ask what you can, Sir,
The obedient tongue won't fail to answer.

And quickly was it done as said,
The Greenback touch was on Bram's head.

CHEEZE.

Hast thou reliance, hope, and trust
In thy own Cheezey ?

BRAM.

Well, I must.

CHEEZE.

Dost think him honest as he's great,
What e'er betide?

BRAM.

         He'd sell the state.

CHEEZE.

Why then by thee is he caressed?
Why not discard?

BRAM.

         'Tis not my interest.

CHEEZE.

How can this be ; art thou content
To leave thy Cheezey to his bent?
You know his object is by paper circulation,
To lay down pipe for next term's nomination—

BRAM—(*interrupting him.*)

Your rhyme's played out, my cove. I ain't no such
fool as to give up this berth to Salmon P. Cheezey or
any other man. I ain't here for nothing, and I just
tell you I 'm going to stay here.

CHEEZE—(*blandly.*)

But the people, my dear Bram, the people. You
know if the people say your time 's up, you must go.

BRAM—(*excitedly.*)

The people be d—d! Do you suppose I 've been
playing the Fool and the Honest Man all this time
for your benefit. No, gentlemen ! 'Tis time we under-
stood one another. The Honest role I have under-
taken was to further my own ends, not yours.

CHEEZEY—(*soothingly.*)

My dear Bram, you know we made you what you are. But for us you would still have been the obscure, uncouth, Illinois rail-splitter, "unwept, unhonored and unsung."

BRAM.

I want to hear no more of this. You nominated me for your own ends. I jumped at the offer and was elected, and sometimes I shudder at the great sin I committed ; for, to be elected, I had to pledge myself to your views and those of Soo, Stentor, and the whole party. Now look at the consequences.

CHEEZE.

But the Union, my dear friend, the Union. You forget that. See the strength of our own party today, by simply changing the name from Black Republican to Union.

BRAM.

Stuff and bosh ! and you know it too. What is all this talk about the Union. You want no Union— neither do the rest. You want what I want, but I'll be hanged if I am going to let you get ahead of me at it.

CHEEZE—(*suspiciously.*)

What do you mean ?

BRAM.

I MEAN EMPIRE ! *That's what I mean, and that's what you mean, and that's what all of you mean ;* but I've got the advantage of you in the race, and intend to keep it.

CHEEZE—(*aside to Soo and Stentor, each with his fore-
finger to his nose.*)

The vile toad! He's wide awake. This comes of
elevating such trash.

STENTOR.

I didn't suspect him of such ideas. It reminds me
of Tittlebat Titmouse and his patron.

SOO.

My friend, suspect every man. No one is too humble to be ambitious—none too 'honest' to take that
which has no owner, and EMPIRE is one of those
things—and none too ignorant to grasp that which
has been thrust at him. Cheezey, suppose we vary
the entertainment by touching him upon the subject
of "Buffoonery."

CHEEZE.

Good. We'll talk about that other matter anon.
[*Advances to the sleeping Bram, and touches his bump of
"jokes."*] What's the biggest joke you ever heard
of, Bram?

BRAM.

Your legal tender!

CHEEZE—(*viciously.*)

Bram, your jokes always put me in mind of a ball.

BRAM.

Why!

CHEEZE.

Because they never have any point!

BRAM.

You never laugh when I say a good thing.

CHEEZE.

Don't I? You'd better try me with one!

BRAM.

When does the House of Representatives present a ridiculous appearance?

CHEEZE.

When it discusses my finance bills.

BRAM.

No. *When its ayes* (eyes) *are on one side, and its noes* (nose) *on the other.*

CHEEZE.

Pretty good. Now tell me why is Dick Busteed like Necessity?

BRAM.

That's old, Cheezey. *Because he knows no law.* But speaking of law reminds me of a good thing I heard the other day on old Breezy Welles. A fellow down in Ohio exhibited him a plan for making ships out of india-rubber. Old Periwinkle wouldn't listen to him, though, because he was afraid that *such ships in crossing the line, might rub it out !*

" The law entitles me to be heard," said the Buckeye.

" Go to Gov. Morgan," said the Secretary.

" But he's your brother-in-law," urged the inventor.

"Then go to Captain So-and-so."

"But he's your nephew."

"Then go to Commissioner So-and-so."

"But he's your cousin."

"Then go to the devil."

"Ah, that's a still closer connection," said the fellow, pitching an inkstand at the Secretary's head and consoling him with the parting reflection that "All's well as ends Welles."

CHEEZE.

You said 'twas not your interest to discard your Cheezey. Have you no fears his power over the treasury will carry him into the presidential chair ?

Soo—*(to Cheeze.)*

You're out of order, Cheezey. He cannot reply to that question. It's not a funny one.

CHEEZE—*(to Bram.)*

Well then Bram, you said my legal tenders were the biggest joke you ever heard of. Ain't you afraid the joke may be carried too far for your chances of re-election.

BRAM.

No. When the time comes I'll put a stop to them. They remind me of a story I heard out west at one time. There was an old farmer who had an old mare called Greenbacks. He took her out one day to plow. But the old mare wouldn't go, no how. He coaxed her and coaxed her, then he whipped her and whipped her, and finally he set his gal SUE at her with a big stick to beat the hide off of her. She wouldn't

go though, and the old man was in a tarnation fix.
"Calkerlate I'll swap the mare off," says he, "or
what's better, I'll sell her to Uncle Sam for cavalry
purposes;" when jist as he was gettin' kinder soft on
her, up she starts and goes off at a canter that threat-
ened to knock the wind out of her in tarnal short
time. After her goes the old man, tumbling over the
furrows, and risking his neck at every step. "Hal-
loa!" says Sue, and she strikes after old Greenbacks,
and runs up to his neck with her cudgel a hitting
him right smart in the *tender* parts. "What are you
about there Sue," said the old man. "Trying to get
that all-fired green-bottled fly off his neck," said Sue.
"Don't do no such thing!" screamed the old man;
"that green-bottled fly is all that makes her go and if
you brush that off she'll bust her biler and collapse
straightway!" Now that green-bottled fly is Cheezy's
hopes for the Presidency. As long as I leave that
on, the machine will run easy, but the moment it is
taken off the critter stops and devil a foot of land will
be reclaimed.

CHEEZE.

Then you believe in Greenbacks?

BRAM.

As I believe in steam. Useful while under control;
but sure to bust up if used expansively.

SOO.

We ought to have old Welles here on the subject
of expansive steam.

STENTOR.

Or Isherwood.   He might give us the benefit of his
Lake Erie experiments.   But let us change the
theme.   What do you say to a touch of biography.

SOO AND CHEEZEY.

Agreed.   Suppose you take him in hand, Stentor.

> 'Twas done.   The crafty Stentor passed the drinks around
> 'Till Abram's slumbers grew the more profound ;
> Then mounting high his categoric stump,
> He tapped Bram's auto-biographic bump.

Chapter III.

BRAM'S BIOGRAPHY.

"I was first elected," commenced Bram, "to the
Illinois legislature in 1834."

"Stop, stop," cries Soo, "if you've no objection
Bramy, we'll go back a little earlier."

"Come, come, gentlemen," said Stentor " you don't
want the man to tell us all his flat boating and wood-
sawing adventures in Illinois."

"Yes we do," said Soo, "we want to know how such
a man ever emerged from obscurity, and in doing so
perhaps elicit some beneficial hint for our private
benefit."

" Well then, I was born," continued Bram speaking still with his eyes closed and between his teeth, as
though against his will " on the 12th of February,
1809, in La Rue county, Kentucky."

"Oh we know all that," interrupted Soo; "your mother's name was Nancy Hanks and your father's Tom Lincoln, a rail splitter, stump extractor, swamp clearer, root burner, and cow breeder."

"That's true," said Bram, "but he was of aristocratic descent.* We can trace our lineage to the times of Robin Hood, who had about him men in Lincoln green."

A sarcastic smile and a movement towards his LITTLE BELL, betokened the rising contempt in Soo's great breast. The others interposing, he resigned himself to Bram's genealogical rhapsody.

One of my ancestors, was the noble Earl of Lincoln, who emigrating to America along with Wm. Penn to escape the displeasure of Charlemagne the great, brought with him a stump of the rod of Aaron and a copy of the *Habeas Corpus*."

"Which you have since lost," suggested Stentor.

"Exactly," said Bram, with a chuckle "which ain't no whar to be found. The first thing they did was to make a treaty with the Indians who were in rebellion against the infant colony and could'nt be put down under ninety days. The treaty was as follows:

' *Motto—The* PENN *is mightier than the Sword :*

ART. 1. The Indians agree to give up all their lands.

ART. 2. All their medicine men.

ART. 3. All their squaws.

ART. 4. Everything else.

ART. 5. And to accept a bottle of bad whiskey in return.'

---

*Barrett's Life of Lincoln, page 11.

"Well, the natives stuck to this arrangement with commendable honor until they got their whisky, when they broke into open revolt. Penn was for peaceable measures, but Lincoln advised coercion. Said Penn, 'you cannot fight always.'*

'But Lincoln showed that if the war was conducted with sufficient ferocity, the aborigines would soon be wiped out and the country would be their own. So they went in and slaughtered without mercy, giving no quarter, making no exchanges, nor sparing even the women, and burning and confiscating everything in their path. In a very short time the country was cleared and Penn and Lincoln not agreeing about a proper division of the spoils the latter with the aid of his soldiery, took the best part of it and leaving the avaricious and envious Penn, settled on the best farming lands and established himself supreme in the western part of the country. His posterity eventually became attracted to the new state of Kentucky and removing their immense capital thence, invested it in the lumber business."

"Not so fast, mighty Bram," cried Soo, "what do you mean by 'capital' and 'lumber business?'"

"Well their capital consisted of a rifle and a broad ax and the lumber business was the trees standing all round them ready to be cut down."

"Rather a falling off," suggested Cheeze.

"They quarreled a good deal with one another, and that was all there was left. My immediate ancestor there met and wooed the lovely Hanks, and in proper time I made my appearance. I grew so fast

*Inaugural.

that my father used to be in the habit of making chalk marks on my legs to see how much I gained over night. He had to raise the top of our shanty on three occasions to make room for my increasing altitude, and even then I had to put my head through the smoke-hole in the roof, to comb my hair.

From Kentucky we moved to Indiana, generously leaving our stock of standing lumber—— "

" Which you couldn't take with you," hinted Cheeze.

" Exactly. Leaving our stock of lumber to the next man that came along, we squatted in Indiana near what is now called Gentryville.* As we were intent upon remaining there, we didn't need a log cabin—— "

" How so?,, asked Stentor.

" Because we were as I said *in tent.*"

" But how did you provide for your farm stock, your pigs and chickens?" persisted his interrogator.

" Well, as for the pigs, we tied their tails in a knot and so provided each of them with a *pigs tie*, and as for the poultry, we inherited our great ancestors' genius for a *coup de etat.*

" The reasons why we left our old Kentucky home I need not go into. Suffice to say in the words of one of my biographers: ' We have at least the fact, that, though painfully, and with an exile's sadness, he turned his back forever on a State that tolerated slavery, to seek a new home where free labor had been sacredly assured exclusive rights and honors.'†

" After receiving my education I was elected to the Illi——"

---

* Barret's Life.   † Barrett's Life, p. 24.

"Stop, stop, stop," cries Stentor, "you appear to be in a great hurry to get to the legislature. Let's hear a little more of your Indiana life. What kind of an education did you get?"

"Well, the first thing I learnt was the dignity of labor.* That consisted in twenty-deck poker, and handling a gad, thus:

> Plowing, sans shoes or socks on,
> With snake pole and a yoke of oxen.

I stumped a twenty acre field with immense success. I learnt my statesmanship from a comic almanac, and got my jokes from an old Joe Miller."

"How long were you at school?" asked Cheeze.

"I'd rather not answer that question, gentlemen," pleaded the sleeping Bram.

"You must!" replied Stentor.

"Well then, about a year altogether.† But you musn't judge me from that. I learnt a good deal from A FRIEND in Illinois."

"If you only went to school a year, what's the meaning of this passage in your 'authentic biography:'

'His *last teacher* was a Mr. Dorsey, who has had the satisfaction, in later years, of taking his former scholar by the hand, rejoicing to recognize the once obscure boy as the foremost LEADER OF THE PEOPLE.' "

"Oh! that meant OFFICE" said Bram.

At this magical word the conspirators were observed to lose their sportive humor and become much more taciturn. Bram continued:

"The name of *honest*, which was afterwards be-

---

* Ibid, p. 24.   † Ibid, p. 25.

stowed upon me by A FRIEND, is popularly attribu-
ted to the following incident of my life :

I borrowed a book from a man named Crawford,
and as books were very scarce in those parts, *I lost
half of it.* Carrying the ruined book to my friend, I
offered to pull fodder for him for two days, to make
it square. As he didn't have any fodder to pull, he
took me, and I pulled it, and so made the matter
square. So my biographer put it in this shape : 'The
offer was accepted and the engagement literally ful-
filled. As a boy, *no less than since* Abraham Lincoln
had an honorable conscientiousness, a constitutional
integrity, a miscellaneous industry, and an ardent
love of knowledge.'

'When I was nineteen years old, I went a flat
boating. Now gentlemen, people are very fond of
calling me a flat boatman, a rail splitter, and so forth.
I assure you I never made but one voyage on a flat
boat † and never split but one rail and that's the *rail*
truth. Pass the bottle over here, Cheezey."

"*Really*, Lincoln," commenced Soo, "you are the
meanest li——."

"Hush," said Cheeze, plying the President with a
gallon of contract whisky.

Chapter IV.

About this time I made the great discovery that
"it is easier to pay a large debt than a larger one.
That it is easier to pay a small debt than a large one ;
and that it is easier to pay nothing than even a small
debt."

*Ibid page 26   † Ibid.

"The events that occurred during my absence, were of such a nature that I deemed another voyage would benefit my health, so I bade good bye to all hands and braved the western wave once more."*

"I thought you only made one voyage!" said Soo.

"The only one at *that time*. Ha! ha! a good joke. Well I made my second voyage down the river and picked up a good deal of money by dancing jigs and singing nigger songs."

"I don't see any notice of that in any of your numerous biographies," interrupted Stentor, referring to a stack of books on the shelves, all labeled, 'Abraham Africanus, his life and services.'"

"Yes," returned Abe, "it's all writ down; only in different language. Just refer to Jim Barret's Life, page 35, and you will see: 'It is reported by his eminent friends that His Excellency refers with much pleasant humor to this early experience, some of its incidents affording abundant amusement to his auditors.'"

"On my third voyage, I sang so much that my jaws have remained widened ever since. On my fourth voyage, I told so many yarns that my neck got stretched over four inches. From some I got the sobriquet of "Clam mouth"—from others that of "Scraggy," perhaps in allusion to the proportions of my neck. On my eleventh voyage—"

"Hold!" cried Stentor "These voyages are getting tedious. There is no end to them."

"There's only one more," replied Cheeze; "then we'll get him on the subject of rail splitting."

"If he's as good at rail splitting as he is at Union splitting," rejoined the warrior, "we shall have some rare amusement. But let us end these voyages. It's evident he has a tedious succession of them to relate for the fool is only *half seas over* as yet."

"Pretty good," said Soo, lighting a cigar, "I agree with you, Stentor. Drop these *flat* boat yarns, and let's have some *rail* anecdotes."

"Agreed, gentlemen," said Bram, "but in leaving the water for the land I'm afraid you find my stories rather *dry*."

"*Tell that to the marines*," cried Stentor.

"Moisten them with a little 'forty-rod,'" suggested Cheeze.

Chapter V.

RAIL STORIES.

"After thirteen voyages, I went in on my old grounds and re-occupied them. I took a laborer with me by the name of Johnny Hanks and we together split 3,000 rails."

"Stop one moment," cries Soo. "How long did you take to split them."

"In a day, I take it," says Cheeze.

"No interruption, gentlemen. I want to get at the truth of this. Well, how long, Abe?"

"About six years!" replied Abe.

"And how many of you were there?"

"There was Hanks, and me, and ——"

----

*Barrett's—page 34.

"Never mind, that'll do. If you can't amuse us without lying, my friend, we'll have to let Cheeze take the chair in 1865, and leave you out in the draft."

"Don't, *don't!* Soo, my friend," cried the sleeping Bram, with sudden energy. "I'll do anything you wish —Let me only be President for four years more! I thought it would be no harm to romance a little. It's so popular with the people; dear creatures, they'll believe anything."

"All very fine, your Excellency," rejoined Soo, "but, just remember you can't stuff *us* quite so readily."

"Gentlemen," said Bram, turning to his auditors one by one and exhibiting his great lanky face blanched with fear and working with petty cunning—"whatever is done, I don't want you to leave me out in the cold. I'd sacrifice everything to be re-elected. I've got a million of money at command and can produce more if wanted!"

"Where from?" asked Cheeze.

"Oh never you mind," replied Abe, with a knowing air. "It's none of your shabby greenbacks, Master Cheeze, but good SOLID GOLD. I've got friends that have the chink, gentlemen."

At the word "gold" they all pricked up their ears. Taking advantage of their attention, Bram broke forth:

"Oh friends of my bosom, I've made up my mind
    And to miss re-election I don't feel inclined,
To you a large fortune I'd gladly give o'er
    If you let me be in office just four or five years more.

Gentlemen, I repeat my request. *Don't* leave me out in the draft. I had enough of that once."

"Let's hear about it," said Sentor.

"Promise to keep me in office, then. Do, my dear Stentor," said Bram with a cringing air, and trying to get on his knees and clasp Stentor's legs, "you know how much I've done for you—made you chief of the war department when you never knew anything of war, given you million after million of profits on contracts—bigger spoils than Cameron ever earned or Morgan and Cummings ever dreamed of; and you, Cheeze, I've given you every chance—you must have made largely on all them revenue cutters, besides what you laid by in gold contracts and stock operations."

The humility of the creature was disgusting. He dragged himself towards Soo and exclaimed in pitying accents:

"Soo, I've given you every chance, kept you in office after your blundering allowed the Sumpter and the Alabama to get out—after you let Mason and Slidell escape—after you gave up the mails of the Peterhoff—after you truckled to every power in Europe and permitted France to ignore the Monroe doctrine. I've let you lock up all your private enemies in Forts Lafayette, Delaware and Warren, and many of them in dungeons from whence they will never emerge. Surely, you can't be so ungrateful as to throw me, after all that?"

The three conspirators began to dislike the turn affairs had taken.

They soothed him, promised him everything, got him in his chair again, and started him on the Subject of the Black Hawk War.

Chapter VI.

The modesty of a soldier forbids that I recount the valorous deeds performed by me during this campaign; this I leave to Barret, whom I have rewarded with a fat office for his pains. On my way back to Illinois, and while separated on the road from my companions, I met and defeated, single handed, twenty of the natives, and left their dead bodies on the road.

"WHAT!" cried Cheeze and Stentor, in stentorian chorus, "Twenty-five—and single handed, too!"

"On my honor," said Bram, with an air of modest merit.

"Oh! oh!"

"Gentlemen, allow me to explain," interposed Soo. "I think I can give you the clue to this in a moment. Meanwhile, let us hear what became of Black Hawk."

Bram thus reminded, continued his tale:

"It seems that TAYLOR came upon him at the bluffs of the Wisconsin, and after one of the most absurd battles ever fought, he defeated Black Hawk and took him prisoner. For the sake of getting hold of this man and putting an end to the war, he absolutely sacrificed several of his own."

"How many of the enemy did he kill?" asked Stentor.

"About sixty-eight. Only think of it. It makes one's blood run cold to think of it"

"Remarkable instance of a sensitive nature," said Cheeze, in a bland tone, putting his fat white hand approvingly upon Bram's head and smiling at his confreres. "Now, Soo, let's hear the sequel of the twenty-five natives killed by my friend, (you'll permit me to call you my friend, Bram?)

"Certainly, Cheezey, here it is. I shall read an extract from a Congressional speech of Mr. Lincoln, delivered during the canvass of 1848."

"By the way, Mr. Speaker, did you know I am a military hero? [Derisive laughter from the galleries.] Yes, sir, in the days of the Black Hawk War, I fought, bled, and came away. Speaking of General Cass's career, reminds me of my own. I was not at Stillman's defeat, but I was about as near it as Cass to Hall's surrender; and like him, *I saw the place very soon afterwards.* It is quite certain I did not break my sword, for I had none to break; *but I often drew the long bow.* If Cass broke his sword, the idea is, he broke it in desperation; I drew my bow for amusement. If General Cass went in advance of me in picking huckle-berries, I guess I surpassed him in charges upon the wild onions. If he saw any live fighting Indians, it was more than I did, but *I had a good many bloody struggles with the mosquitos,* and on one occasion I remember to have *killed twenty-five of them single handed!*"

"This, gentlemen," said Soo, is a verbatim extract from the *Daily Globe;* and what is more it was in this momentous struggle the great Bram first realized that immortal saying—"Nobody Hurt!"

Chapter VII.

PALMAM QUI MERUIT FERAT.

Bram felt so indignant at the laughter raised by this sally of Soo, that he refused to answer any more questions. The Confederates petted and soothed him to no purpose. He was as obstinate as a mule.

Soo then proposed, in order that the amusement should not flag, to continue Bram's biography from Barret's pages, and meanwhile Stentor should ply the sleeper well with 'forty rod,' until he got him in good humor again. This being agreed upon, and Bram well nourished with the 'star-spangled-striped-pig,' Soo opened the book, and commencing at page 47, read:

"We now approach the period in the life of this exalted personage which he was destined by nature to attain—we mean the career of a statesman. Still it must not be concealed that Mr. Lincoln's own preferences were in favor of a military life. The adventurous career he had just passed through in the desolating warfare with Black Hawk, and the heroic deeds which make his name illustrious in the annals of the State of Illinois, in connection with this now famous campaign, made him feel that Providence had not intended him to be a mere private in the great battle of life, but that he had certain qualities which could place him at the head of a column, or of a brigade, if he were so minded.

He came home from the Black Hawk War with the high and noble determination of working for his own living thereafter, provided he would get nobody else to do it for him.

His tact at wire pulling, his acquaintance with the long shore men and other roughs of the place, and his faculty of sticking at nothing to gain power, obtained its legitimate reward, in his election to the State Legislature.

He was so exhausted of funds after getting into the legislature that his *surveying instruments* were sold under the hammer.

His appearance in the legislature was not very dignified it is true—but he made up for that by the quickness he soon displayed of making money. He possessed the rare art of assuming an extra uncouthness or rusticity of manner and outward habit, for the purpose of securing particular favor with the masses

He seldom or never spoke during the session, but found means to have himself appointed on the Committee of Public Accounts and Expenditures, which he managed so well that nobody ever suspected him·

On both subsequent occasions that he was elected to the Legislature—he always managed to get himself on Committees that had the management of Money Affairs—and in this respect showed obvious wisdom.

He had thus (p. 63) honorably acquitted himself on the battle-field, in defending our border settlements against the ravages of the savage foe, and in the halls of the legislature had an eye to the main chance.

His eloquence was so scathing and withering, that that which at first would appear plain and probable, he made to look crooked as a serpent's path ; and that which was tortuous and involved, he straightened out and made it plausible to the simplest minds.

This talent stood him in so well, that when in 1860, the Presidential Convention met at Chicago and gave on first ballot, 173 votes for Seward, 50 for Cameron, 49 for Chase, 48 for Bates, 14 for Dayton, and 12 for McLean, he managed matters in such a way, that on the second, Cameron's name was not voted for, and on the third, he (Lincoln) got the nomination himself by 231 votes. It is said he rather got the best of both Seward and Chase."

"Fool!" cried the Premier, throwing away the book and *touching his little bell*, "I'll teach the knave to write us simpletons, eh, Cheezey?"

"Fool," said Cheeze.

An officer entered.

"Search for a man named Barrett, who wrote a life of Lincoln and convey him under a strong guard to Fort Lafayette! No charge. Instruct Col. Burke not to obey writs of *Habeas Corpus*."

"Excuse me, your honor," said the officer, "but if I'm not mistaken this same gentleman you refer to is one of the President's ministers now on foreign stations."

"What political services did he perform to deserve that post," demanded the lofty Soo.

"He wrote that very book, your worship," replied the marshal.

"Ah I see. You may go."

The officer retired.

The Confederates looked serious. This little incident alone, convinced them they had no child to deal with. Bram was evidently up to snuff. And when they came to think for what a small mess of pottage they had bargained away their own nominations, they wondered how this flat boat-man of long shanks and little brains had managed to outwit them all.

All three fell into a brown study.

Chapter VIII.

THE FRIEND.

A long time elapsed before either of them spoke.

It was a singular scene. Upon a chair reclining at his greatest length, his feet upon the hearth, his hands in his pockets, his head resting heavily on his chest, his hair dishevelled, his cravat awry, and a general air of smuttiness, and a general odor of liquor pervading him, sat Bram ; still dreaming, still snoozing, still in the mesmeric state, and yet so strong in his self concentration, so fixed in his self estimation, as to be capable of being indifferent, in spite of his stupor, at the exposure his own words had made of his ridiculous boasts and his miserable inconstancy.

There sat Soo, turning the keys over in his trousers pocket, thinking what a fool he had been to lift such a man into power, and at his own expense, and to his own great shame.

There Stentor, too, weighed uneasily the poor chances that remained of his longer holding office, and stretching his legs out under the table, put one hand to his waist-coat arm, and with the other fumbled at his watch guard.

Cheeze lustily rattled a pocket full of specie (he

was the only one that had any hard money about him, though the others didn't lack paper,) and passed the time with glancing uneasily at his three companions, probably distrustful of them all.

Stentor was the first to break silence.

"Soo," said he, "tell us a story to while away the time."

"Don't ask me, Stentor, my boy, I've told so many different stories in my time, and none of them seemed to answer, that I despair of ever succeeding with another. Ask Cheezey to give you a song. He has a fine rich voice, sweet as a syren's. He sung so sweetly to the New York bankers two years ago, that they haven't got over it yet."

Cheeze, thus called upon, begged to be excused—said he was no singer—only knew one song, and didn't like to sing that on account of its disunion tendencies—and so on.

"Pooh, pooh," said Soo and Stentor in a breath, " we don't care anything about its disunion tendencies, as you call it. You don't suppose we are such asses as to believe in the political nursery trash we preach, do you?"

"It's a *nursery song*," said Cheeze.

"Go ahead, then, my boy," said Soo.

Stentor nodded an additional approval, and thus fortified, Cheeze cleared his bag-pipe and thus began :

Air.—*A Song of Sixpence.*

Sing a song of Greenbacks,
  Pockets full of trash,
Over head and ears in debt
  And out of ready cash ;
Heaps of Tax Collectors,
  As busy as a bee ;
Ain't we in a pretty fix
  With gold at sixty-three.

Bram in the White House,
  Proclamations writing ;
Meade on the Rapidan
  Afraid to do the fighting,
Seward in the cabinet
  Surrounded by his spies ;
Halleck with the telegraph
  Busy forging lies.

Cheeze in the treasury,
  Making worthless notes ;
Curtin at Harrisburg,
  Making shoddy coats ;
Dahlgren at Charleston,
  Lost in a fog ;
Forney under Bram's chair
  Barking like a dog.

Schenck down at Baltimore,
  Doing dirty work ;
Butler at Norfolk,
  As savage as a Turk ;
Sprague in Rhode Island,
  Eating apple sass ;
Everett at Gettysburg,
  Talking like an Ass.

Banks out in Texas,
  Trying to cut a figure ;
Beecher in Brooklyn,
  Howling for the Nigger ;
Lots of Abolitionists,
  Making such a yell,
In comes Parson Brownlow,
  And sends them all to hell.

Burnside at Knoxville,
  In a kind of fix ;
Gilmore at Sumter,
  Pounding at the bricks ;
Grant at Chattanooga
  Trying Bragg to thrash :
Is it any wonder
  The Union's gone to smash ?

" Bravo ! bravo !" *encored* the friends. " Cheezey,
my boy, you've a mellow voice and a fine vein of humor."

" You'd say, I had altogether too much humor if
you knew, how cheaply I let that countryman there,"
pointing to Bram, " *chouce* me out of the nomination on
last election," returned Cheeze, secretly flattered at
the compliment, but chagrined at the reflections it
suggested.

At these words, Soo began to pick his teeth.
Stentor commenced spitting tobacco juice at a key
hole.

"It seems to me as though that man had the DEVIL
at his side," continued Cheeze.

Soo here arose from his chair and advanced
towards Cheeze.

" Cheeze," said the Secretary, "I have the same
belief myself and I have more than one reason for
it."

Stentor who had been crossing himself with pious
vehemence now got up and turning to Cheeze, said:

"And I, too, have heard strange stories about
Bram's Friend."

"And I," chimed in Cheeze. " Suppose we ex-
change ideas and tell each other what we know about
it."

To this they all agreed, and resuming their old
postures, they first wet their whistles, then satisfied
themselves that Bram was still unconscious, and Soo,
setting the example, began telling what he knew of
Bram's Mysterious Friend and Patron.

Chapter IX.

DEVILISH STRANGE.

"I have heard it related by a party that Mr. Lincoln has seen fit to incarcerate in Fort Warren, that on a certain occasion when Bram was very hard up, and had to sell his furniture out there in Illinois, in order to keep the pot boiling, he wandered out into the prairie, unconscious of where he was, so deeply was he engrossed with the difficulties that beset him on all sides. He hadn't a friend in the world, and didn't know what to turn his hands to, to earn a living. Thus moodily engaged he came near to a spot where my informant was trapping prairie hens, and then he sat down and gave vent to his pent up miseries in these words:

"Calkerlate I'd better bust these parts and emigrate right smart, or maybe I'll come to grief Mother's cove in and father's looking arter other critters; flat-boatin is too all-fired fatiguing, rail-splitting is played out, 'cause Hanks throwed me, and singing nigger songs is gone to smash. I could dance right smart on a spring board; but what's the use when you can't get nuthin' for it but a shock or two o' corn and a pull of forty rod. I'd a heap sight rather go a canallin' if I could git aboard one of them craft; but even them is no go. There ain't no canals in this section of the country. 'Taint no use speculatin' on father's kickin' the bucket, so the only thing left is to dig a hole here in the prairie, and just expire right off."

So saying, he proceeded to divest himself of his

clothing and boots. The latter he hung up on an old ridge pole that stood on the plain and affixed a placard to them. They were odd specimens of foot gear, being nearly eighteen inches long and proportionately wide; the legs or uppers were so near the centre, that it was difficult to determine which the wearer had the most of, heel or toe, and the soles were entirely gone from long wear. The placard read thus:

"These is from Abe Hanks, likewise named Abe Linkun, to the widder Hennepin, her son, likewise named Abe. The eels is fled, the shanks is rather *gone up*, the soul is gone *the other way*, but the uppers is good, and will make a pare of boots four him if he's a good boy. Fairwel! my biler is bust, and go I must.   ABE HANKS.

And now, said the intended suicide, making a pillow of his clothes, and lying down on the earth in a posture of determined sleep, "I don't care what the *devil* becomes of me."

He had no sooner said the word DEVIL, than up jumps a man as it were from the very earth itself, and advances very politely towards the recumbent Abe. In a few moments they became very intently engaged in conversation, but in such low tones that my informant could not catch a word.

Curiosity getting the better of judgment, he crept cautiously towards them until he heard the stranger say:

"On this condition, sign the bond and you shall not only get all you ask but I'll make you a member of the Legislature.

"What!" cried Abe, "Have you any interest with the Legislature."

"I should think I had," returned the other "I'm personally acquainted with every man of them, and besides that, keep a boarding house *down below* for all the ex-members."

"Suppose I stir up this all-fired nigger question, kinder cussed brisk, what'll you do in that case, old boy?"

"Keep you in for two terms."

"Could'nt you make it Washington instead of Vandalia," insinuated Abe.

"What!" cried the other. "Are you so ambitious as all that? Why, man, you haven't ability enough to keep two listeners in their seats."

"Never mind that" returned Abe. "Just you help me a little when I falter, and have the name of "Honest" well stuck to me, and I'll go through it easier than you imagine."

"Well then, agreed," said the other, "and if any success attends the plan, and any certain indications of civil war appear, I will be willing perhaps to enter into a new contract with you. *You know war contracts are very profitable.*"

"What do you mean?" enquired Abe, evidently not understanding his friend correctly.

"I mean *I'll give you the first contract under the war.* YOU AGREE TO BRING TO DEATH ONE MILLION OF HUMAN BEINGS; and I'll agree to give you the Presidency.

'THE PRESIDENCY!' exclaimed Abe, rising from the earth in his agitation, and seeming to soar with his long limbs, as high as the ridge pole itself. His emotion was so extraordinary, that words failed to express it. The stranger pleased at this exhibition, extended his hand. Abe grasped it heartily, and pulling the other towards him, threw himself into his arms. They were the tallest pair my informant ever saw, and bore a striking resemblance to each other—sufficient to be brothers. Fearful of discovery, he crept away at this juncture, and turning round at the distance of a couple of miles, beheld them still together, standing hand in hand beside the ridge-pole."

Chapter X.

THE FIEND.

The last words of Soo's tale died away into a sort of hoarse whisper, and were heard in dead silence; as the supernatural subject of it fixed itself upon the minds of himself and his listeners.

A long silence followed it.

Soo whittled the arm of his chair, Stentor poked the fire, and Cheeze pulled out a little parchment scroll from his vest bosom and read it over privately; glancing at the others now and then to see if they were watching him.

"All right," he murmured, "it doesn't interfere with *my* contract. Every man for himself, say I."

At this moment a knock was heard at the door.

"Come in," said Stentor.

The door flew open and a servant in livery disclosed himself.

"The President?" he enquired blandly.

"Not here," returned Soo curtly.

"Excuse me, my Lud—I mean your Excellency—

but if I'm not mistaken, the President is before me."

"I tell you he's not here," persisted Soo.

"And I tell you, you lie!" roared the flunkey, pushing past him and rousing the sleeping Bram from his chair.

Soo became livid with rage.

He ran to his *little bell* and hastily put his name to a blank order of arrest. An officer appeared at the door.

"Here!" said he, "arrest that impudent rascal directly, and convey him to the vilest dungeon in America."

"Where?" enquired the officer.

"Park Barracks, New York."

The officer advanced and collared his prisoner.

"Come along with me," said he roughly.

But Bram was now fully awake and seeing the danger his Cockney friend was in, quickly interposed his superior authority.

"Let go!" he commanded.

The officer relinquished his hold.

"*Vamous!*" said Bram.

The provost marshal obsquatulated the ranche.

"What's all this about, gentlemen;" said Bram furiously, "can't a friend of mine ask for me without running in danger of being arrested?"

"The Confederates hung their heads without daring to say a word. Bram glared furiously upon them.

"How long have I been to sleep," he demanded.

"Nearly three hours," replied Cheeze.

"Have I been blabbing to you—saying anything I ought not to have said—been indiscreet? Eh?"

Rapid glances passed between the three. Bram

caught one of these tell tales, and suspecting all was not right, changed his tone instanter.

"Pardon me, Soo, my boy, I was only joking with you. Let's make up. I'll give you permission to lock up the very next man that comes along.* Cheezey and Stentor, I'll make it all square with you when I come back. We'll make up a game of poker, *and play one Southern plantation ante up.* How do you like that? eh?"

"Capital!" they exclaimed.

They shook hands all around, and looked quite delighted; and in the midst of all this happiness, Bram departed, arm-in-arm with his liveried friend. As the door closed upon him, the faces of the Confederates lengthened.

"Who is that flunkey?" asked Stentor, "that Bram should feel so soft about him and be so thick with him?"

"Is it possible you don't know?" replied Cheeze.

Stentor shook his head.

"Nor do I," jerked out the mortified Soo, "or I wouldn't have handled the fellow so roughly. Pray enlighten us."

"He is the private and confidential servant of Doctor ———," and here Cheeze whispered the name in his friends' ears.

Soo looked serious. Stentor didn't comprehend it.

"Who is doctor ——— " he began, bluntly.

"Hush!" said Cheeze. "Don't mention the name for worlds. I'll tell you. Did you never hear of a certain Chiropodist in New York who possessed great

---

*This very next man happened to be Dr. Ives of the New York *Herald*, afterwards of the *News*.

mastery over Bram's mind—who could manage him any way he pleased—who cut his corns—went on secret missions—was commissioned to New Orleans to watch Banks and afterwards to Norfolk to overlook Butler—who possessed great influence with all the rich Jews in New York and undertook to get loans of money from them—the H-n-d-r-cks, the J-s-phs, who used to represent the Rothschilds, the B-mh-m-rs, the E-nst-n-rs, and the N-th-ns?—who got up the Russian Ball, and who danced with Mrs. Bram, at the party last winter?—who doctors him, and writes his speeches?—who advises him and directs him in questions of state? who——

"Hold!" cried Soo, "I thought I was the man who did all this!"

"The devil you did!" cried Stentor, "I thought I was the man."

"You're both wrong, gentlemen. *I* was the man till the doctor stepped in and took the wind out of my sails, for which I was not sorry, for I was getting tired of him at that time, and might have missed the opportunity, I soon after had, of forming an alliance with another party."

Soo and Stentor bit their lips till the blood came, and then ran from the room howling, [French style.]

Cheeze smiled complacently and sitting down to the table, penned the following telegram in secret cypher to New York:

"Buy Rock Island at anything under 140 for a 'corner.' Sell 2,000 Erie 'short' and bull the market on gold. Mum."

Chapter XI.

A YEAR LATER.—THE END.

How little do the humble know,
What miseries greatness is heir to,
What heart-aches, jealousies and cares,
Beset their anxious hearts with fears,
When high resolves have once elated,
What pain to see them all frustrated.
What hellish passions take their place,
When failure brings with it disgrace ;
How stoop their minds beneath the blow,
To everything that's mean and low,
What shifts they make, what agents use,
What'er gives hope they madly choose.
With naught to risk, they spare no cost
To gain position they have lost ;
Debased themselves, they seek to find,
A kindred baseness in mankind.
And feeling self-condemned the while,
Would think all others just as vile.

'Twas eve of one eventful day,*
As story tellers always say,
The President had far surpassed
His greatest effort and his last ;
And all the world went home in thought,
On all the wondrous things he taught.
The day had passed—the crowd had gone,
And all that had been said or done,
Were records of the silent past.
Say, will his fleeting triumph last?
The fierce excitements of the day,
Had chased the great man's griefs away ;
But now, when all was calm again,
Began the torments of his brain,
And in his silent chamber, there

---

*The eve of the 1st of November, 1864.

Awoke the vision of despair.
No longer from his fishy eye,
Shot cunning and shone energy ;
But lone and silent, and subdued,
He yielded to his sullen mood.
Long time he sat, convulsed and wrought,
Till words gave utterance to his thought.

" Oh! what a wretched thing am I,
The veriest fool of destiny ;
How meanly have I sunk below
The dignity of honest woe.
How have I lost that high estate
I might have held among the great,
And sunk beneath my own approval,
Condemned myself to cringe and grovel ;
I grasped at POWER ; *fool, fool!* the thought
Now mocks the ruin it has wrought.—
Time was when even foes respected,
But now how fallen and neglected ;
The stake was POWER for which I cast,
'Twas but its shadow, and it passed ;
My friends betrayed—I fondly bowed,
To woo the passions of the crowd ;
But failing there, I sought again
My former standing to regain.
All will not answer, on my sight
The future rises to affright,
And in that future will I mark
A path as devious and as dark !"

———————

Air—*Brilliante Posterioso.*

The Devil took sick,
The Devil a saint would be ;
The Devil got well,
The *devil* a saint was he!

"Ha!" cried listening Bram, "'tis thou,
Well hast thou timed to tempt me now!"

And sure enough, polite and civil,
There stood our laughing, friendly Devil,
Who with his usual courtly grace,
Smiled sweetly in the great man's face,
And with his cloven foot before him,
Bowed very low in all decorum.
"Nay, there you wrong yourself !—not swerve you ;
But doing all I can to serve you."
So *sweet* he smiled, and bowed *so* low,
The great man thanked ; what could he do ?

"Thanks! thanks!" great Bram replied,
For Satan had aroused his pride,
And in the presence of the devil,
He wish'd t' appear at least as civil.
"If I had doubted, let it pass,
Henceforth I'll be no whimpering ass,
But, faithful to myself and you,
Be firm in what I think and do !"

"Bravo!" cried Satan, "'tis well said,
And worthy of your heart and head ;
But tell me—if I don't offend
Why can you ever doubt me, friend ?"

" Why thus it is : I see too clearly
Why friends are falling from me daily.
The more I strive, the more they fail me,
While foes on every side assail me."

"Nonsense," quoth the fiend, " where's your pride?
Great men like you, ar' n't cast aside ;
With little power to do you evil,
They'll court you yet, or I'm no Devil."

"Have I not striven night and day,
To lead opinion my own way,
And used the powers of wealth and station
To gain the good will of the nation—
And to what end ? except to grieve me :
The very knaves I fed, deceived me."

"Patience!" cried Satan, "patience, kind Sir,
Your very hurry makes you blind, Sir.
Where's your NIGGER PROCLAMATION,
That bitter bolus for the nation,
And your CONFISCATION BILL?
Think you THAT inflicts no mischief still?
Think you that each demagogue forgets
That novel way to pay war debts?
When gazing on your empty coffers,
He sees the prospects which it offers.
Think you he sees not hereabout,
A very fine way to get out,
And chuckles as he fondly eyes,
Repudiation in disguise?"

"Zounds!" quoth the great man with a start,
"I tell thee, Devil though thou art,
This bantering tone 's all very fine,
But one thing at least 's no plan of mine.
I'm speaking of the Greenback—Pshaw!
I mean the repeal of the Homestead law."

"All mighty well," quoth Satan, grinning,
How very coy you are, while sinning;
But I, who know your modest way,
Will not object to what you say,
And all the less, most faultless brother,
Since all the world now blames another.†

But ne'er the less it works MY ends
And cannot make *us* else than friends.".

Bram, who though at first astonished,
Smiled as Satan thus admonished;
Smiled as he saw his views displayed,
In what the Devil shrewdly said
Smiled as he saw himself unmasked,
And thus of Satan, smiling, asked :—

---

† Thurlow Weed, in February 1864, in a letter to Ex-Gov. Morgan of New York,
cooly purposes to repeal the Homestead Law, and sell the public lands to foreigners
to pay the war debt.

ABRAHAM

Who serves the Devil,
Devil take him ;
But will the Devil
E'er forsake him ?

"No," cried the Old One of a sudden,
"This jest of yours is not a bad 'un,
You would by joke assume superior,
Whereas, in fact, you are inferior.
And being servant, aye, *don't stir, Sir !*
You must obey ; *a slave you are Sir.*
A slave you are, and though much bigger,
As much a slave as any nigger.
A slave you are, because you'll cheat,
And therefore, you are mine complete.
A slave you are, and now believe me,
You cannot, if you would, deceive me ;
In all that does relate to sin,
I give the power, you but take in."

"Nay, nay, Your Darkness, pause awhile,
My joke was made to raise a smile ;
But since it was misunderstood,
I'll recommence in sober mood."

"'Tis useless," quoth the Devil, bowing,
I feel 'tis time I should be going ;
Give me thy hand ; for, Bram, thou art
In thought and art my counterpart ;
So like; that if (could such things be,)
You had been kicked from heaven with me,
We *snacks* had gone—yes, who can tell
And kept a hotel down in hell.
I see you like the joke—you laugh,
But time is up. I must be off,
Yet e'er a friendly leave I take,
I've fancy for a hearty shake."

The great Bram seized the proffered hand,
But—had he grasped a lighted brand,
His quivering nerves and changing look
Had not such sudden torture spoke.
He strove to free his hold—but no,
That scorching grasp would not let go.

*   *   *   *   *   *   *   *   *   *

Thus, on the very day before election,
The Devil claimed his great connection ;
And hurling Bram to black damnation,
At last relieved the Yankee Nation.

THE END.

THE

WASHINGTON DESPOTISM

DISSECTED,

IN ARTICLES FROM THE

METROPOLITAN RECORD.

CONTENTS.

134 PAGES.   PRICE 25 CENTS.

J. F. FEEKS,

PUBLISHER,

No. 26 Ann Street, New York.

NOTES

ON THE

CONSTITUTION OF THE UNITED STATES,

CONTAINING THE

TEXT OF THE CONSTITUTION,

WITH

EXPOSITIONS

Of the Most Eminent Statesmen and Jurists; and

Historical and Explanatory Notes

ON EVERY ARTICLE,

WHEREIN MORE THAN SEVENTY VIOLATIONS OF THAT SACRED
INSTRUMENT, ON THE PART OF THE ADMINISTRATION,

ARE POINTED OUT & CLEARLY PROVED.

BY

C. CHAUNCEY BURR,

Author of the "HISTORY OF THE UNION AND THE CONSTITUTION."

Price, in Paper Covers, - - - 25 Cents.
" Cloth. - - - - - 50 "

J. F. FEEKS, PUBLISHER,

26 Ann St., New-York.

IN PRESS:

LINCOLNIANA;

OR THE

Humors of Uncle Abe.

SECOND JOE MILLER.

" That reminds me of a little story."—PRES. LINCOLN.

PRICE—Paper, · 25 Cents. Cloth, · 50 Cents.

J. F. FEEKS,

Publisher,

26 Ann Street, New York.